Fables   Fables

en   in

Deux Langues   Two Languages

et   and

Divertissements   Similar

de Ce Genre   Diversions

Fables en Deux Langues et Divertissements de Ce Genre

Fables in Two Languages and Similar Diversions

Charles W. Pratt (signature)

POEMS BY *Charles W. Pratt*

PICTURES BY *Marian Parry*

POMME PRESS

BRENTWOOD, NEW HAMPSHIRE

1994

The author thanks Laurent Patenotte, André Vernet and others who have helped bring his erratic French more into line.

Some of this work (play) has previously appeared in *Light Year '86, Light Year '87, Sometime the Cow Kick Your Head: Light Year '88/9* and *Light.* "L'Oiseau, la Souris, et le Chat"/ "The Bird, the Mouse, and the Cat" was first published in *In the Orchard* (Tidal Press, 1986).

The poems of others are from the following sources: *Fables de la Fontaine,* Lambert Sauveur, ed., Philadelphia, John Wanamaker, 1877; Victor Hugo, *Les Contemplations,* Paris, J. Hetzel & Cie., 1891; Arthur Rimbaud, Poésies Complètes, Paris, Léon Vanier, Libraire-Editeur, 1895; Charles Baudelaire, *Les Fleurs du Mal,* Paris, Calmann-Lévy, Editeurs, 1868.

Designed and manufactured in New England for
Pomme Press, 66 Rowell Road, Brentwood, NH 03833.

To friends on both sides of the Atlantic with whom
we have shared the happy adventure of approximation, and
à vous, aimables lecteurs—nos frères—nos sœurs!

He who binds to himself a joy
Does the winged life destroy;
But he who kisses the joy as it flies
Lives in eternity's sun rise.

—WILLIAM BLAKE

Vive la différence!

Matières · Contents

L'Oiseau, la Souris, et le Chat

Un petit oiseau chantait
Sous le soleil de mai—
«Qu'il fait beau, qu'il fait beau, fait beau!»
Une souris lui chuchota,
«Ne sais-tu pas que le chat
Cherche par-ci, par-là,
Un morceau tendre comme toi?
Les petits doivent se taire. C'est la loi!»
L'oiseau chanta encore plus haut—
«Qu'il fait beau, qu'il fait beau, fait beau!»
Un jour vint le chat et mangea
Notre ami l'oiseau. Voilà,
Plus de chansons dans les champs,
On n'entend que le clac-clac des dents.
Et puis le chat prit la souris
Malgré les bons conseils soumis;
Il la mangea, c'est bien dommage,
Bien qu'elle fût silencieuse et sage.
La leçon qu'on apprend—qu'est-ce que c'est?
Qui ne chante jamais, ne chantera jamais.

· 8 ·

The Bird, the Mouse, and the Cat

A little bird warbled away,
  Gay in the sunlight of May—
"What a day, what a day, day, day!"
"Psst!" hissed a mouse. "Keep it low!
Mister Pussy's out prowling, you know.
He's quite keen of hearing, and oh!
How morsels like you make him drool.
The small must keep still. That's the rule."
The bird sang still louder, "Hooray!
What a day, what a day, day, day!"
One morning, along came the cat
And caught our friend bird. That was that.
A muffled chomp-chomp, and done!
No more songs in the sun.
And next the cat ate—it's not nice—
Despite all its careful advice,
The mouse—popped it into the hopper,
Though so perfectly silent and proper.
The lesson you'll learn, if you're clever?
If you don't ever sing, you won't ever.

Le Loup Végétarien

Louis le petit loup
Ne mangeait jamais que des choux.
Il ne trouvait pas du tout bon
Le plus joli gigot de mouton,
Ni le blanc de dindon,
Le filet mignon,
Le ragoût.
Mais il faisait des loopings de loup
Pour la moindre feuille de chou.
«Vaut mieux manger du veau,»
Maman l'implorait. «Un morceau?»
Ses soeurs marmonnaient, «Bizarre,»
En bouffant du steak tartare.
Papa crevait de chagrin:
«Hein! Je suis père d'un lapin?»
Mais Louis: «A chacun son goût,»
Et il allait chercher des choux.

The Wolf Who Wouldn't Eat Meat

Cabbage was all that wee Willie Wolf would eat—
Never meat.
Not a lambchop, no matter how tender; not the least chew
Of turkey, steak, stew.
But so rabid for cabbage was Willie the tiniest bite
Induced a wolf-whoop
And a wild loop-the-loop
Of delight.
"A nice slice of veal's a much healthier meal,"
  His Mom in vain would appeal.
"Weird," his sister'd guffaw,
  Wolfing down hamburgers, raw.
  Dad would blow up. "The disgrace!
  A son who's a bunny. I can't show my face
  At the club." But Willie: "There's no accounting
  For tastes." And he'd go cabbage-hunting.

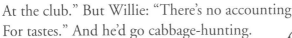

Le Chien Libre

Charlie le chien
N'exige rien
Ni écoute
Aucun appel.
Il suit sa route
Le nez au ciel
Ou le nez à terre,
Mangeant de l'air
Pour faire du vent
Ou des pierres
Pour se casser les dents.
Son bien-être
Cherchant sans maître,
Il chasse sa queue
Au lieu d'un dieu.
Je m'appartiens,
Pense Charlie le chien;
Je vais très bien
Sans laisse ou lien.
Je m'en irai
Quand j'en aurai envie,
Et je ne manquerai
A nul ami.

FREE DOG

Charlie Dog begs no bone
And doesn't answer to anyone.
Nose in the sky he rambles along
Chewing on air for a windy song,
Or nose to the ground chewing on stone
To break his teeth. All alone
And masterless, he finds his trail,
Chasing no god but his own tail.
Charlie Dog thinks, all of me's mine;
Without leash or chain I do just fine.
I'll be on my way when I'm so inclined,
And no friend or lover to notice or mind.

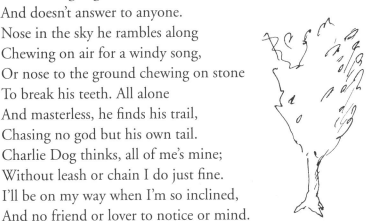

Le Moustique Mystique

Le moustique mystique,
Attention à lui—
Quand il pointe sa pique
Vers sa victime choisie
Ni filet ni écran
Ne détourne son élan.
Il n'a pas envie
De boire du sang,
Il se moque des pique-niques
Les dimanches au printemps;
Il vise l'esprit
De l'homme en tourment!
Au lit à minuit
Sans espoir de repos
Vous l'entendez vrombir
Dans l'abîme du cerveau;
Vous l'entendez vrombir
Et vous savez son nom:
Le moustique mystique

Vrombissant sans trêve
Même dans vos rêves
Son éternel Om!
Comment gifler
Cet insecte épineux?
Inutile d'essayer.
Comment gratter
L'esprit galeux
Du péché, du chagrin?
Rien ne le peut,
Ni les drogues, ni le vin.
Le moustique mystique,
Attention à lui!
Quand son murmure amer
S'étouffe enfin
Et qu'il met dans l'étui
Son aiguille de fer,
C'est tout, mon ami,
Et vous payez le prix
Dans la glace de l'enfer.

THE MYSTIC MOSQUITO

Beware of the bite
Of the mystic mosquito,
Whose missile-like flight
No defenses can veto;
The warm taste of blood's
Not his sort of thing,
He never invades
Sunday picnics in spring;
He has just one goal:
To torment the soul.
Imagine it's midnight,
You're tossing in bed
In sleepless despair;
In the cave of your head
You hear something hum
And you know that *he's* there,
He's not incognito,
The mystic mosquito,

Who hums and who hums,
Hums in your dreams
His unceasing Om!
Is there no way to smash
This meddlesome bug?
No wine nor drug
To soothe the soul's rash
Of guilt, regret, sorrow?
No, again no.
The mystic mosquito,
Oh, listen to him!
When his anguishing hum
At last has been hushed
And his bitter-tipped blade
Put away in its case,
It's finished, my friend,
And the price must be paid
In deepest hell's ice
Time without end.

Mon Petit Poulet, Adieu

Mon petit poulet, rond et roux,
Pond de grands oeufs de caoutchouc,
De caoutchouc de bout en bout.

Les autres poulets, fort jaloux,
Hissent la queue et poussent, fous:
Des oeufs ordinaires, c'est tout.

Moi, ce sont ces oeufs que je veux.
On ne peut pas manger des pneus.
Mon poulet rond et roux, adieu.

FAREWELL, MY LOVELY

My favorite hen, so plump and tender,
Fluttering fire in every feather,
Lays big eggs of solid rubber.

The other hens, in jealous frenzy,
Hike up their tails and push like crazy,
But all their eggs are ordinary.

Such are the eggs that I require.
No one can eat a scrambled tire.
Farewell, plump bundle of fluttering fire.

L'Huître Snob

De Locmariaquer, l'huître,
En lampant le vin par le litre,
S'expliquait, «Se soûler
Au meilleur Muscadet,
Voilà ce que l'on doit à son titre.»

Le Concombre Triste

J'ai connu un vieux concombre
D'un tempérament plutôt sombre;
«Triste, triste,» disait-il; «C'est mon sort
De pendre à l'ombre jusqu'à la mort.»

The Hoity-toity Oyster

The oyster of Locmariaquer,
  Downing wine by the jug would declare,
"I'm obliged by noblesse t'
  Drink only the best
  Muscadet till I fall from my chair."

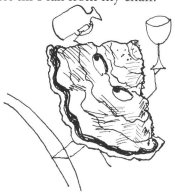

The Sorrowful Cucumber

My old friend the cucumber's soul
  Was what you'd call glum, on the whole;
"My doom, too, is gloomy," he said:
"To hang in the shade until dead."

La Truie Qui Pratique le Zen

La truie qui pratique le Zen
Tout le jour médite, sereine.
Pleine de foi, elle attend
Son repas de glands.
(Elle pratique le Zen sous un chêne.)

THE ZEN SOW

All day the Zen sow meditates serenely
Waiting for nutfall
Under the oak.

Histoire

Quand les petits nuages
Sont arrivés à la plage
Tous les enfants sont rentrés.
Les petits nuages ont pleuré.
Croyez-vous que c'est dommage?
Ainsi les fleurs ont été arrosées.

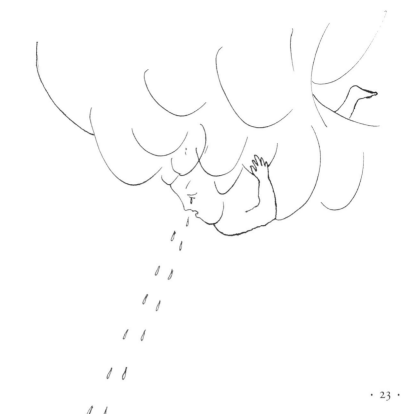

STORY

When the little clouds came out to play
The little children went away.
The clouds cried. Sad, you think?
The flowers, however, were glad to get a drink.

Le Papillon et l'Ordinateur

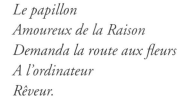

Le papillon
Amoureux de la Raison
Demanda la route aux fleurs
A l'ordinateur
Rêveur.

«Des cartes à l'écart
Prenez votre départ
Des règlements
Du monde du ciment
Armé;
Suivez
L'impulsion du vent
Vers le soupçon
De l'odeur
D'une couleur . . . »

«Pourquoi vous faites
Le poète?
Je cherche une cervelle.»

«Et moi, des ailes.»

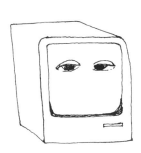

The Butterfly and the Computer

A butterfly wanting to Know
Asked a dreamy computer how
To find the flowers.

"Forget the orders of the orderly mind;
Leave behind
Maps and magistrates,
The strict dictates
Of straight streets,
Concrete walls.
The wind calls;
Follow
Its slim
Whim
Towards the scent of yellow . . ."

"Poetry gives me a pain.
Speak plain.
What I need's your brain."

"And I,
Your wings to fly."

Le Breton Romanesque

«Les Fleuves m'ont laissé descendre
où je voulais» — Rimbaud

C'était André Lelabourier,
Le brave garçon, le bon Breton,
Qui courbait le dos vers la terre
Pour en tirer de quoi manger
Pour lui et pour sa vieille mère.
Mais il voyait dans les noirs sillons
L'éclat de la Méditerranée.
Ce bon Breton, ce brave garçon,
Retournait des vers de Baudelaire.

Les soirs, en regardant la soupe,
—Le brave garçon, le bon Breton—
Qui bouillonait dans le gros pot,
Il y trouvait la Guadeloupe
Comme un mirage sur le flot
(Ce n'était, peut-être, qu'un oignon),
Et il se voyait sur la poupe,
Ce bon Breton, ce brave garçon,
Du bateau ivre de Rimbaud.

Il aurait aimé suivre Gauguin,
Le brave garçon, le bon Breton,
En voyageant à Tahiti,
Cette île romanesque et loin
Des pommes de terre et de la pluie
De la Bretagne; hélas, non,
Fidèle il restait dans son coin,
Ce bon Breton, ce brave garçon,
Pour faire son boulot à lui.

Un jour sa sage mère lui dit,
«Mon brave garçon, mon bon Breton,
Va-t-en, cherche ton Paradis
A la Guadeloupe, à Tahiti.
Si tu y es déçu, tant pis.
Plein d'usage et de raison
L'oiseau au soir recherche son nid,
Mon bon Breton, mon brave garçon,
Mais tôt le matin il est parti.»

C'était André Lelabourier,
Le brave garçon, le bon Breton,
Qui partit pour le Paradis,
D'où il revint accompagné
D'un être joli et bruni.
La sage mère: «Entrez, donc!»
«Que vous partiez, que vous restiez,»
Dirent ces braves, ces bons Bretons,
«Le coeur chez soi c'est le Paradis.»

The Romantic Yankee

"I have traveled widely in Concord" —*Thoreau*

There once was a fellow named Richard Brown—
New England stock, solid as rock—
Who busted his back sunup to sundown
To scratch enough food from one poor field
To keep his old mother's platter filled.
But the gleaming black furrow folding back
From his plow had a Mediterranean glamour.
This solid rock, New England stock,
While he turned the worms was rehearsing Homer.

Often at night he'd sit and stare—
New England stock, solid as rock—
Into the bubbling stewpot where,
Like a mirage above the foam,
Rose up a white and mystic form—
A potato playing Moby Dick?—
And he'd dream that he was drifting off in
(This solid rock, New England stock,
Had read his Melville) Queequeeg's coffin.

He was no stay-at-home like Thoreau—
New England stock, solid as rock;
He longed to go search for El Dorado
Or some Pacific paradise
Far from New England snow and ice
And wormy apples. But he stuck,
Faithful, to his meager plot,
Solid as rock, New England stock,
Doing the job that was his lot.

One day his wise old mother said,
"You're New England stock, solid as rock,
But go on, travel. Once you're dead
You'll never see what there is to see.
The Orinoco. Greece. Tahiti.
If it's a let-down, no big shock.
You can't go home again, they say,
And my solid rock, New England stock,
They're right, if you've never gone away."

Brown took his mother's sound advice—
New England stock, solid as rock—
And set right out for Paradise,
Whence he soon returned to the farm
With a brown angel on his arm.
His mother: "Happy to have you back."
"Whether you stay or whether you roam,"
Said these New Englanders, solid as rock,
"Paradise is the heart at home."

Ressusciter un Mort

Mais oui: le cheval est mort,
Définitivement.
Mais le vieux gars lève le bras
Et le bat, et le bat,
Et le bâton le bat, le bat—
Bon, bah, bon, bah, bon, bah—
Contre la peau
De celui qui était une fois peut-être
Un pur sang
Mais maintenant
N'est que des os
Dans un sac de cuir,
Une baleine sur la plage
Echouée, gonflée de gaz.
Moi, je veux lui dire
«Viens, il te faut faire
Du stop;
Il y a plein de voitures sur la route.»
Mais le vieux gars lève le bras et bat,
Et bat,
Comme s'il battait le tambour
D'un grand défilé
Le jour de la Bastille.
Et le cheval lève la tête, il frémit, il se met debout.
Et le vieux gars lui empoigne la crinière, il se lance à bord.
Et ils sont partis.

Beating the Dead Horse

No doubt about it: the horse is wholly dead,
But the old guy's arm keeps flailing up and down
And the stick keeps whamming its monotonous
Dumb bah dumb bah dumb against the hide
Of what may once have been a thoroughbred
For all I know, but now is scrambled bone
In a leather bag, a beached-whale load of gas.
So why not stick out a thumb and hitch a ride,
I want to ask; plenty of cars on the road;
But the old guy's arm keeps flailing up and down
As if he were beating the drum in some glorious
Fourth of July parade.
                      The dead horse lifts its head,
Shudders—rises; he grabs it by the mane
And leaps aboard. Suddenly, they're gone.

La Diva

Un jour en pêchant dans la Seine
Je rencontrai une baleine,
Ses grands jets d'eau
Jouant en haut
Comme le chapeau d'une reine.

Sous sa proue un trait de blanc
Semblait sourire gentiment
Aux bateaux
Autour dans l'eau
Et aux arbres sur les bords se courbant.

Le long de ses flancs, l'eau luisante
Coulait comme la soie glissante—
Ma foi, qu'elle
Etait belle,
Grande, noire et élégante.

«Pardon, madame,» enfin j'offris,
«Est-ce que vous allez à Paris
Pour chanter à
L'Opéra . . . ?»
Elle inclina la tête—oui.

«Pardon, madame, encore pardon,
Mais veuillez chanter une chanson?
J'espère que—
Je lis dans vos yeux—
Vous aimez partager votre don.»

Elle chanta donc, n'importe quoi,
Le monde chanta avec sa voix
Résonnante,
Ravissante,
L'eau, la terre, le ciel et moi.

Elle chanta haut, elle chanta bas,
Elle chanta quelque aria.
Tous les oiseaux
Crièrent—Bravo!
Battant des ailes pour la Diva.

Le long de ses flancs, l'eau luisante
Coulait comme la soie glissante—
Ma foi, qu'elle
Etait belle,
Grande, noire et élégante.

Sous sa proue le trait de blanc
Semblait sourire gentiment
Aux bateaux
Autour dans l'eau
Et aux arbres sur les bords se courbant.

· 33 ·

THE DIVA

Walking down Fifth Avenue one day,
Just looking in the store windows, imagining,
When along comes this black lady
All dressed in silk, sleek and shiny as the Hudson at night,
And hair piled up on top of her head—way up, like a crown—
A real queen,
And smiling like a queen.
My god, she was something!
All the people on the sidewalk stopped and looked at her,
And the cars on Fifth Avenue stopped,
And the drivers stopped swearing and snarling
And just sat with their mouths open and stared,
She was so grand
And so black
And so—smooth.
Excuse me, lady, I said finally,
Excuse me,
But are you an opera singer on your way to the Met?
That's it, I bet.
And she nodded, still smiling.
Excuse me again, I said,
Excuse me, lady,

But maybe—
You look nice—
You'd sing us something?
So then she sang, I don't know what,
And everything sang with her voice,
Echoing,
Ecstatic,
The streets, the buildings, the sky, and me.
She sang high,
She sang low,
She sang some aria, I guess,
Until even the taxi drivers shouted "Bravo!"
And honked their horns,
This grand black lady
All dressed in silk, sleek and shiny as the Hudson at night,
And hair piled up on top of her head—way up, like a crown—
A real queen,
And smiling like a queen.
My god, she was something,
So grand
And so black
And so—smooth.

Le Chêne et le Roseau

Le chêne un jour dit au roseau:
Vous avez bien sujet d'accuser la nature;
Un roitelet pour vous est un pesant fardeau:
Le moindre vent qui d'aventure
Fait rider la face de l'eau
Vous oblige à baisser la tête;
Cependant que mon front, au Caucase pareil,
Non content d'arrêter les rayons du soleil,
Brave l'effort de la tempête.
Tout vous est aquilon, tout me semble zéphyr.
Encor si vous naissiez à l'abri du feuillage
Dont je couvre le voisinage,
Vous n'auriez pas tant à souffrir:
Je vous défendrais de l'orage;
Mais vous naissez le plus souvent
Sur les humides bords des royaumes du vent.
La nature envers vous me semble bien injuste.
Votre compassion, lui répondit l'arbuste,
Part d'un bon naturel; mais quittez ce souci:
Les vents me sont moins qu'à vous redoutables;
Je plie, et ne romps pas. Vous avez jusqu'ici
Contre leurs coups épouvantables
Résisté sans courber le dos;
Mais attendons la fin. Comme il disait ces mots,
Du bout de l'horizon accourt avec furie
Le plus terrible des enfants
Que le nord eût portés jusque-là dans ses flancs.
L'arbre tient bon; le roseau plie.
Le vent redouble ses efforts,
Et fait si bien qu'il déracine
Celui de qui la tête au ciel était voisine,
Et dont les pieds touchaient à l'empire des morts.

Jean de la Fontaine

HEROIC OAK; THINKING REED

Oak spoke:
"Cruel joke
It was indeed
Nature played
When she made
You, puny reed.
A bird's a burden you bend under;
If a whiff of wind should pass,
Just enough to ruffle water's glass,
You bow, humble,
While my brow I proudly raise,
Not satisfied with catching rays,
Like McKinley to the rumble
Of the thunder—
Brave the blast.
What to you's a gale to me's
Mere breeze.
If you'd been born in the protectorate
That my leafy arms create,
You'd have less cause to curse your fate;
I'd rebuff wind's blowhard bluster.

But you're bred in that moist zone
Where wind rules the roost alone.
Nature couldn't be unjuster."
Reed replied,
"Sir, you're kind
To have me so much on your mind,
But you're much more at risk than I;
I ply,
But I don't break. You've defied,
Stiff-backed, wind's worst this far, that's certain;
But wait until the final curtain
Drops." He spoke,
And from the belly of the north there broke
The fiercest wind-child ever sent
Out howling to harry earth. Reed bent,
And oak was oak.
The wind-child blew; it blew again; it blew
So hard at last it overthrew
That tragic one who brushed the sky with his head
And whose roots reached down to the country of the dead.

after la Fontaine, «Le Chêne et le Roseau»

La Coccinelle

Elle me dit: Quelque chose
Me tourmente. Et j'aperçus
Son cou de neige, et, dessus,
Un petit insecte rose.

J'aurais dû, — mais, sage ou fou,
A seize ans on est farouche, —
Voir le baiser sur sa bouche
Plus que l'insecte à son cou.

On eût dit un coquillage;
Dos rose et taché de noir.
Les fauvettes pour nous voir
Se penchaient dans le feuillage.

Sa bouche fraîche était là;
Je me courbai sur la belle,
Et je pris la coccinelle;
Mais le baiser s'envola.

«Fils, apprends comme on me nomme,»
Dit l'insecte du ciel bleu,
«Les bêtes sont au bon Dieu,
Mais la bêtise est à l'homme.»

Victor Hugo

LADYBUG

Oh, it's more than I can bear,
She declared—and so I searched
Her snowy neck, and found there
A little rose-red insect perched.

I should have—yes, but tell me this,
At sixteen, who's *not* a goat—
Seen the lips that pursed to kiss,
Not the insect at her throat.

You'd have said a shell, may be,
Rose, with inky polka dots.
The warblers in the apple tree
Warbled, will he, will he not?

Her sweet mouth was pouting, so.
I leaned over—breathed her scent—
And caught the ladybug; but oh!
Missed the kiss—away it went.

"God protects the innocent,"
 The insect said, as off it flew,
"But not if they can't take a hint;
 What bugs a lady's mugs like you."

after Victor Hugo, «La Coccinelle»

Ma Bohème (Fantaisie.)

Je m'en allais, les poings dans mes poches crevées;
Mon paletot aussi devenait idéal;
J'allais sous le ciel, Muse! et j'étais ton féal;
Oh! là là! que d'amours splendides j'ai rêvées!

Mon unique culotte avait un large trou.
—Petit Poucet rêveur, j'égrenais dans ma course
Des rimes. Mon auberge était à la Grande-Ourse;
—Mes étoiles au ciel avaient un doux frou-frou

Et je les écoutais, assis au bord des routes,
Ces bons soirs de septembre où je sentais des gouttes
De rosée à mon front, comme un vin de vigueur;

Où, rimant au milieu des ombres fantastiques,
Comme des lyres, je tirais les élastiques
De mes souliers blessés, un pied près de mon coeur!

Arthur Rimbaud

BEATNIK DAYS

I'd hit the road, fists through the holes in my pockets;
My jacket, too, was airy—imaginary.
Out there under the sky, Muse, you were my cherry,
But oh, the hot tickets that sizzled my noggin like rockets!

The seat of my one pair of jeans had a couple of tears.
I scattered my rhymes like seeds as I moseyed on through,
Nutty Tom Thumb. Stayed at the Dipper. The view!
My stars did a little softshoe in the ballroom upstairs

While I sat by the side of the road, turned on and tuned in,
Those sweet September nights when the dew kissed my skin
Till I'd spin as if I'd toked a whole joint of the best,

And I pulled my rhymes from the shadows—it was crazy, I swear—
And plucked my old Nike laces, a sort of guitar,
My ragged old Nike, nestled next to my breast.

after Rimbaud, «Ma Bohème»

Le Chat

Viens, mon beau chat, sur mon cœur amoureux;
     Retiens les griffes de ta patte,
Et laisse-moi plonger dans tes beaux yeux
     Mêlés de métal et d'agate.

Lorsque mes doigts caressent à loisir
     Ta tête et ton dos élastique
Et que ma main s'enivre du plaisir
     De palper ton corps électrique,

Je vois ma femme en esprit; son regard,
     Comme le tien, aimable bête,
Profond et froid, coupe et fend comme un dard,

     Et des pieds jusques à la tête,
Un air subtil, un dangereux parfum,
     Nagent autour de son corps brun.

Charles Baudelaire

BAUDELAIRE

Come pretty kitty, come Baudelaire,
My poetic cat, Mr. Sex Appeal,
Curl on my lap a while while I stare
In your eyes of agate, your eyes of steel.

Put up your claws and let me caress
Your elastic back, your electric fur;
Oh, my hand is drunk with happiness,
Oh, which of us has begun to purr?

It's as if I looked into the eyes of my wife,
For her look is like yours, *cher* Baudelaire,
It's deep, it's icy, it cuts like a knife,

And from toe to head she seems to wear
A coffee aura, a dangerous musk
Cloaking her body like the dusk.

after Baudelaire, «Le Chat»

THE ALMOST BALLADE OF THE *Rennes d'Aujourd'hui*

Nous avons vu l'ombre du Mont Saint-Michel
Bénissant les eaux de la haute marée;
Nous avons vu les grands vitraux de Chartres
Saignant en rouge et bleu sous le soleil;
We've played at boules and baseball on the beach,
And shivered in the autumn rains of Rennes;
We've made new friends and talked to them of old,
And started planning how to come again.

We've lost and found ourselves on twisting streets,
And bought patisseries and Muscadet;
We've watched the changes of a foreign sky,
And thought of friendly places far away;
Nous sommes allés tels des soldats à l'école,
Où tout le monde regarde les étrangers;
Nous avons espéré et essayé,
Et quelquefois, tout seuls, nous avons pleuré.

Nous nous sommes promenés à la campagne,
Cherchant des mûres, des pommes et des châtaignes;
Et quand nous sommes rentrés, main dans la main,
Nous savions que le voyage en vaut la peine;
We've gone to market, counting our francs and French,
And searched for a plumber on a Saturday;
We've read, made maps, written long letters home,
And felt the weight of all we couldn't say.

We've felt the weight of all we couldn't say,
Et quelquefois, tout seuls, nous avons pleuré;
Nous savions que le voyage en vaut la peine,
And started planning how to come again.

FABLES IN TWO LANGUAGES AND SIMILAR DIVERSIONS
has been printed by Conway Lithograph in an edition of
1500 copies. The text is printed on acid-free Mohawk
Vellum Warm White and the jacket on Mohawk Ultrafelt.
Marian Parry drew the illustrations in pen-and-ink.
Bruce Kennett designed the book and typeset it in Adobe
Garamond. This 20th century type family is based on the
letters used by the great French typographer Claude
Garamond during the first half of the sixteenth century.

Fables en Deux Langues et Divertissements de Ce Genre à
été tiré en 1500 exemplaires par Conway Lithograph. Le texte à
été imprimé sur Mohawk Vellum Warm White, non-acide, et
la couverture sur Mohawk Ultrafelt. Marian Parry a dessiné
les illustrations à l'encre. Bruce Kennett à achevé le dessin du
livre et il a fait la typographie en Adobe Garamond. Cette
"famille typographique" du 20e siècle à été dérivée des carac-
tères d'imprimerie employés par Claude Garamond, le grand
typographe français du 16e siècle.

References

Bowermaster, J. 1981. *Classroom management and learning in elementary schools.* Champaign, Ill.: Educational Resources Information Center.

Caldwell, B. M. 1977. Aggression and hostility in young children. *Young Children* 32: 4–13.

Combs, A. W. 1962. A perceptual view of the adequate personality. In *Perceiving, behaving, becoming: A new focus for education,* pp. 50–64. Washington, D.C.: Association for Supervision and Curriculum Development.

Cousins, N. 1979. *Anatomy of an illness.* New York: W. W. Norton and Co.

_____. 1981. *Human options.* New York: W. W. Norton and Co.

Dreikurs, R. 1964. *Children: The challenge.* New York: Hawthorn Books.

Dreikurs, R., and P. Cassel. 1972. *Discipline without tears: What to do with children who misbehave.* New York: Hawthorn Books.

Dreikurs, R., and L. Grey. 1968. *Logical consequences.* New York: Meredith Press.

Elkind, D. 1970. *Children and adolescents.* New York: Oxford University Press.

_____. 1980. Keynote speech, National Association for the Education of Young Children, San Francisco.

_____. 1981. *The hurried child.* Reading, Mass.: Addison-Wesley Publishing Co.

Erikson, E. 1963. *Childhood and society.* 2d ed. New York: W. W. Norton and Co.

_____. 1968. *Identity, youth, and crises.* New York: W. W. Norton and Co.

Fraiberg, S. 1959. *The magic years.* New York: Charles Scribner's Sons.

Gould, R. 1978. *Transformations.* New York: Simon and Schuster.

Haswell, K. L., E. Hock, and C. Wenar. 1982. Techniques for dealing with oppositional behavior in preschool children. *Young Children* 37: 12–18.

Katz, L. 1977. Teachers in pre-schools: Problems and prospects. *International Journal of Early Childhood* 9: 110–23.

Kounin, J. S. 1970. Observing and delineating techniques of managing behavior in classrooms. *Journal of Research and Development in Education* 4: 62.

Maslow, A. H. 1962. Some basic propositions of a growth and self-actualization psychology. In *Perceiving, behaving, becoming: A new focus for education,* pp. 34–49. Washington, D.C.: Association for Supervision and Curriculum Development.

Mead, M. 1972. *Blackberry winter.* New York: Simon and Schuster.

Osborn, D. K., and J. D. Osborn. 1981. *Discipline and classroom management.* Athens, Ga.: Education Associates.

Phyfe-Perkins, E. 1981. *Effects of teacher behavior on preschool children: A review of research.* Champaign, Ill.: Educational Resources Information Center.

Rogers, C. R. 1962. Toward becoming a fully functioning person. In *Perceiving, behaving, becoming: A new focus for education*, pp. 21–33. Washington, D.C.: Association for Supervision and Curriculum Development.

Satir, V. 1972. *Peoplemaking*. Palo Alto, Calif.: Science and Behavior Books, Inc.

Silverstein, S. 1974. *Where the sidewalk ends*. New York: Harper and Row.

Sutton-Smith, B. 1975. Keynote speech, Chicago Association for the Education of Young Children, Chicago.

Yawkey, T. D. 1980. Creative thinking and self-concept in young children. In *The self-concept of the young child*, ed. T. D. Yawkey, pp. 151–63. Provo, Utah: Brigham Young University Press.

Index